Leadership Secrets of David the King

Bob Yandian

*Penny
Thank you for being
a blessing
[signature]
Isa 33:6*

Leadership Secrets of David the King
ISBN: 1-885600-27-5
Copyright © 1995 by Bob Yandian
Bob Yandian Ministries
PO Box 55236
Tulsa, OK 74155

Published by Harrison House Publishers
Tulsa, OK 74145

Printed in the United States of America.

Table of Contents

Chapter Four   53

Chapter Five   65

Chapter Six   83

Introduction

THE PSALM OF DEGREES

Dynamite Comes In Small Packages

As a young boy raised in church, I was challenged in Sunday school to read a chapter from the Bible every day. Like many of my friends, I would look for the shortest chapters and psalms. Then when asked the next week in class if I had read my chapters, I could comfortably say, "yes." One of my favorite short scripture sections in the Bible is contained in Psalm 131 because it has only three verses. It is one of fifteen consecutive short psalms (Psalm 120-134) called the "psalms of degrees." They represent quite a break in length from the previous psalm, Psalm 119, which has 176 verses. The expression, "dynamite comes in small packages" certainly applies to these short passages of David.

Often, more serious Bible students have overlooked these psalms for the same reason I wanted to read them: they are very short. "If they are short," they say, "they must be insignificant." But since**...All scripture is given by inspiration of God, and it is profitable...** (2 Timothy 3:16), there must be more to these "psalms of degrees" than the last minute postscripts or fleeting thought that came to David.

Bible writers have many thoughts concerning the "psalms of degrees." Some believe they could have been sung on the journey back to the promised land after the Babylonian captivity. Others say they were possibly sung on each of the fifteen steps ascending Solomon's temple, which was a type of the millennial temple spoken of in Ezekiel 40:22, 31. But most think they were "pilgrim songs" sung by the tribes on their way up to Jerusalem for the many annual holy feasts.

Whatever the different thoughts, all agree these fifteen passages are the "gradual psalms," because they represent movement toward a goal or destination. The destination could be a promised land, an annual feast, or as it was for King David, a specific goal in life. Because these psalms are meant to be read by all people in every generation, they are of tremendous value to us today.

We may not be ascending a mountain to Jerusalem, but we are all, as believers, climbing the steps of spiritual maturity. We all know this comes one step or level at a time. Spiritual growth is **precept upon precept**, line upon line, here a little, and there a little. (Isaiah 28:10) But we often become impatient in the Christian life and want to "arrive" by tomorrow morning. Sometimes we become frustrated at the slowness of movement in our walk with the Lord and want to come to our spiritual destination in one step.

We forget God's admonition to us that **the steps of a good man are ordered by the Lord...** (Psalm 37:23), and that nothing after salvation in our Christian life comes in one step. It comes in many steps.

Our natural as well as spiritual growth comes by "degrees." Even the spiritual growth of Jesus occurred as He grew physically. **And Jesus increased in wisdom and stature...** (Luke 2:52) So as you can see, you are in good company.

When a television reporter is interviewing a famous person, he often asks them to give the secret of success that keeps their family together and them sane in the middle of a hectic lifestyle. Often, bits of wisdom from parents, famous authors or coaches have stayed with them for years that formed the foundation on which they based their success. This is what the psalms of degrees are, bits of David's wisdom learned over many years of rulership.

In this book, I will deal with only one of David's "psalms of degrees," Psalm 131. Its three verses may seem rather short, but the psalm is packed with the secrets of David's kingly success that it took him years to gain. The wisdom contained within it will help you in your ministry, home, business and personal life.

The questions most asked of me as a pastor of fifteen years are not about how I started, but how I have continued since then. Some ministers are interested in my time off, vacations, time with my wife and children, and personal study habits. They want to know how these are kept in perspective with a growing congregation and staff. Many of these leaders have found that obtaining power was not as difficult as maintaining it. It is much like finding a luxury car on sale and then finding out the bad news was saved for last: **maintenance and insurance**.

Psalm 131 gives us David's secret of not only obtaining power, but even more importantly, it gives us his secret of maintaining it. David was a man who began as a young boy with a few sheep in the countryside and ended up as a king over millions of people. He faced personal sin, rebellion by his sons and close friends, and a multitude of enemies inside and outside of his own nation. Yet through those many years, he never lost his poise, relaxed attitude, or sense of humor. In Psalm 131 David is saying, "I am just a shepherd boy with a crown." He had learned the attitude of service and humility that makes one great.

Leadership Secrets
of
David the King

Preface

There are only a few things in life that really bother me. One of them is a person who keeps unnecessary secrets. You want to know the reasons behind a leader's success, but he simply won't tell you. It is sad, but behind the tough façade of many leaders beats a heart of insecurity. They believe that by sharing their secrets, they will lose their share of a crowded market. They are afraid you might become great also and crowd them out. They don't understand the scriptural principle you gain by giving. Because this is true, many leaders die with their secrets intact leaving those behind them without the knowledge that brought them to such great levels of achievement.

King David was not that type of leader. Since God keeps no leadership secrets, neither did David. David was as free to share his heart with us as God was to share His heart with David. David would have liked every king to be as successful and happy as he was. In fact, his psalms still teach us how to be kings over every area of life today.

Most of David's psalms tell of the goodness of the Lord and teach us principles of praise and worship. Mingled within them are words of insight from

David's heart. These psalms reveal the leadership secrets that David had learned over many years.

David was no ordinary king. Next to Jesus Himself, he was the greatest king God ever appointed to the throne. Even Solomon, Hezekiah and Josiah were commanded to walk in David's footsteps. After his death, God would use David as an example for Israel's leadership for centuries to come. As you will learn in coming chapters, David was a king of kings.

The purpose of this book is to teach you David's secrets of leadership. There are four principles David taught that could turn your life, your business, and your home around. After you learn them, you could even find people coming to your door to learn these secrets of success.

In other words, *you too can become a king of kings.*

I want you to notice I did not say *The King of kings* – this is a title for Jesus only. But I did catch your attention, didn't I? A king of kings is a boss of bosses, a father of fathers, a mother of mothers, a leader of leaders – in every area of life. A king of kings takes the principle of leadership to the furthest extent. Once you learn David's principles, you will no longer be a student. You will become a teacher, not only through the words of your mouth, but through your daily actions, and more importantly, through your attitude. You will become a living example.

Would you like God to use you as an example for your family and other leaders for generations to come as He did with David? I will go no further. This is the purpose of the book.

Chapter One

The Story of a Traitor

Psalm 131
A Song of Degrees of David

L ord, my heart is not haughty,
Nor my eyes lofty.
Neither do I concern myself with great matters,
Nor with things too profound for me.

2 Surely I have calmed and quieted soul,
Like a weaned child with his mother;
Like a weaned child is my soul within me.

3 O Israel, hope in the Lord
From this time forth and forever.

The losses of a winner are only temporary, so are the victories of a loser.

Psalm 131
A Song of Degrees of David

(*maalah*-advancements) of David

The Truth Behind Inspiration

Peter tells us that the writers of the Word of God...**spake as they were moved by the Holy Ghost.** (2 Peter 1:21) We often have a picture in our mind of the writers of God's Word as either working or relaxing at the end of the day, when suddenly, the Holy Spirit moved upon them. Somewhere we have gotten the idea they had to drop whatever they were doing to spend the next few hours writing Scripture. We think Isaiah, Moses or David had to be ready at a moment's notice to write at the Holy Spirit's whim. Although this may have been true at times, it certainly was the exception and not the rule.

Most of the Bible's writing came as a result of events that happened to the nation or to the writers during their lifetime. As the Holy Spirit taught a lesson from the event, inspiration would come to write. Many of the superscriptions above David's psalms

14

tell of the events that inspired their writing. Psalm 3 speaks of David's divine protection; Psalm 18 of his thanksgiving for God's marvelous blessings and so on with Psalms 30, 34, 51 and 52. Most of the prophets wrote their books describing future prophetic events based on recent personal experiences, events such as famines, pestilences and wars.

Ziba and Mephibosheth

Like many of the other psalms, Psalm 131 was written by David after observing an event in his kingdom. Many of his people had come through the transition from Saul's reign to his. Some were true to David, but others were not. Many were out to truly serve David. Others were after personal gain.

In 2 Samuel 9, we have the story of Mephibosheth. David still had a large parcel of land to give to the line of his friend Jonathan who was killed with his father, Saul, on Mount Gilboa. He went about looking for anyone who was heir to Saul. It is here we are introduced to a seemingly willing servant of the new king, Ziba (pronounced ZEE-ba). Although the main character mentioned in 2 Samuel 9 is Mephibosheth, Ziba will be found behind the scenes in three passages. We are introduced to Ziba in 2 Samuel 9:2-

15

11; told of Ziba's wicked plot in 2 Samuel 16:1-4; and of his fate in 2 Samuel 19:24-30.

Ziba had been the director of Saul's estate for years and had survived the bloody transition of the kingdom. After hearing of David's search for an heir to Saul, he volunteered to find one and brought the son of Jonathon, Mephibosheth, to him. Mephibosheth had been handicapped at an early age. While fleeing from David's invasion, a nurse dropped him, crippling his feet. Mephibosheth's fear of David and his embarrassing physical condition led him to live a life of seclusion. He lived apart and alone, unaware of the true nature of David or the estate that rightfully belonged to him.

Once Ziba revealed Mephibosheth's whereabouts and David sent for him, David treated Mephibosheth with great grace. First, he ate each day at David's table. Secondly, he was given a great estate and all of the wealth that went with it. Finally, Ziba, along with his fifteen sons and twenty servants (foremen), were made to serve Mephibosheth and the needs of his estate.

But David didn't know of Ziba's evil heart. He had risen in position under Saul using his evil schemes and managed to stay alive when David occupied Jerusalem. David didn't know that Ziba had been insulted and angry by the position given him. Not only had Ziba lost his position with the former king, but now he had to be a servant to Saul's crippled grandson. So he worked for seventeen years beside Israel's new king and schemed to steal Mephibosheth's estate. Finally, his chance came with the rebellion of David's son, Absalom.

Ziba's Plan

When Absalom's revolt became known to David (2 Samuel 15:13), the rebellion and insurrection had been four years in the making. Still, David was taken by surprise. Not knowing the extent of the rebellion, or who he could trust, he decided to leave Jerusalem. He needed time to pray for God's will and to regather those who were loyal to him. As he was leaving Jerusalem, Mephibosheth went to saddle his mule. Ziba met him and persuaded him not to go. Ziba had apparently convinced him that his crippled condition would only slow David and his troops. He then volunteered to ride out to meet David himself, to tell him that Mephibosheth would not be coming. He also took food, water and provision for David's long ride. (2 Samuel 16:1-4)

When David was met by Ziba, he was surprised to see him and asked why Mephibosheth had not come. David was especially leery of Ziba because of not knowing who was for him in the rebellion, and who had taken Abalom's side. Therefore, even though Ziba had brought many provisions, David questioned his intent. Ziba assured David he was behind him and the food and provisions were his token of support.

Then, in a moment of weakness, David dropped his guard. Ziba sensed this and lied about Mephibosheth. Ziba told David that Mephibosheth had taken Absalom's side, and this was the reason he had not ridden out to meet the king. He also told David that Mephibosheth was waiting for the entire kingdom to be returned to Saul's heirs after Absalom took the throne.

Without waiting to confirm Ziba's story, David took Mephibosheth's entire inheritance away and gave it to Ziba. Ziba had an ability to separate friends by causing doubt. His ability to "play both ends against the middle" kept him alive during the transfer of the kingdom. David had probably been warned about Ziba by those who were close to him, but sadly he didn't heed their warnings and believed lying Ziba instead. Jesus warned us, **Judge not according to the appearance.** (John 7:24), but this is what David did.

David was so honorable that he believed the same quality was in everyone he met and mistakenly transferred his own integrity to Ziba. Ziba, on the other hand, had charged honest Mephibosheth with his own greed. What he told David of the heart of Mephibosheth was in his own heart. This deceiver had stolen Mephibosheth's estate and the heart of the king with one lie. It would take David many months to finally hear Mephibosheth's side of the story to find out the truth.

The Truth Is Revealed

There is an old parable, "God has given us two ears to hear both sides." When the insurrection was over and Absalom was dead, David rode back to Jerusalem to resume his reign. As the king approached his home, he was met by Mephibosheth (2 Samuel 19:24-30). The young man had not shaved since David had left. Neither had he bathed, washed his clothes, or taken care of his crippled feet. Mephibosheth had done this in support of David and in protest against Absalom. For months he had come to Absalom's table as a disgrace to his household. He openly defied Absalom and became a strong weapon for David during those difficult months.

When David saw Mephibosheth as he came out to meet him, he asked why he had not ridden with him and his men. So Mephibosheth told David how Ziba had met him at the stables and how he had told him it would be of no use to go. He also told David how he himself had been lied to, and that he knew Ziba had lied to David about him. By his unkempt appearance, David knew he was telling the truth. It was then that David finally saw the true heart of Ziba. Now he knew Ziba was a deceiver and a slanderer, and he would stop at nothing to obtain gain for himself. He also did not think a thing about hurting innocent people but would lie to them and steal their possessions. David had been used to take land from an innocent man and give it to a thief.

A Different Mephibosheth

This man that had met him was not the same man who was brought to David as the remaining heir of Saul. Mephibosheth had been a fearful man who let his handicap overcome him, but David's act of grace and kindness had brought about a change in Mephibosheth. The seventeen years he had been a landowner brought him to a great dependency on the Lord. Although he was still crippled in his feet, he was no longer crippled in his heart. He had become very self-confident and gracious toward his master David and the others. David's example before him had made him a different man.

Mephibosheth's maturity came out as he met David. David had believed a liar, and had been deceived by a malicious, arrogant traitor. What was worse, David did not discern this or wait to investigate the story. Mephibosheth would have had every right to be angry, and would have been justified. Yet, he told David the facts and let David make up his own mind.

Mephibosheth did not whine, or beg for the return of his estate. Neither did he remind David of his handicap or play to his master's sympathies. This would have been a return to his days of immaturity. Instead, he trusted David's judgment and fairness and let David make the decision.

But David had his mind made up before Mephibosheth finished speaking. He would not have to think this over. As quickly as David had made a wrong decision, he now made a right one.

Ziba's Judgment

It is here David made a choice that seems difficult for us to understand. Yet it points out the maturity of character that David possessed. Probably our first thought would have been to restore all of the land back to Mephibosheth. We would then search the land for Ziba and hang him along with his servants and sons. We would have had scripture and God's permission on our side. Or, possibly, if our heart would not have been filled with that much vengeance, we would have put a foreman over Ziba and lowered his position on Mephibosheth's estate.

But David divided the estate equally with Mephibosheth and Ziba. Even though David had been deceived, he had given his word to Ziba. He had also given his word to Mephibosheth seventeen years earlier. He found himself in a dilemma. If he would have taken the estate away from Ziba totally, he would have had to share part of the blame. Why? He had believed Ziba's story without investigation.

An example of this is given in Joshua 9. A group of people, the Gibeonites, came to Joshua with tattered clothes, worn out shoes and moldy bread, and convinced him they had come from a far country. They told Joshua they had heard of his conquests and they did not want to be destroyed with the enemies of the land. Joshua told them they had nothing to fear because they were outside the land given by God. They asked for an agreement from Joshua, and without investigating their story, Joshua gave them a treaty and sent them on their way. A few days later, Joshua discovered they lived only a short distance from where they met him. He had been deceived by one of the enemies of the land. He had given his word. It seems Joshua had every right to break his word, since he had been deceived, yet he shared part of the responsibility. Joshua honored his agreement not to invade their city, and the Gibeonites became servants to Israel from that day on. They would not die with the other Canaanites. They would cut wood and draw water for generations to come. Their descendants served Israel into the days of Solomon and worked in the temple doing exactly what Joshua had said.

David knew after seventeen years, Mephibosheth had developed both naturally and spiritually, but that Ziba had become worse. For the many years following Saul's death, Ziba let his anger turn him into a bitter man as he had plotted to take the estate for himself.

Although Ziba had won, he actually lost. And though Mephibosheth had lost, he actually had won. Just as the losses of a winner are only temporary, so are the victories of a loser.

Job 20:5:

That the triumphing of the wicked is short, and the joy of the hypocrite but for a moment.

For years, Mephibosheth would rejoice over what he had gained. But for those same years, Ziba would turn bitter over what he had lost.

Even after the inheritance was divided, the heart of Mephibosheth toward David was clearly seen. He had apparently lost interest in possessions. The true issues of life had become most important to him – his relationship with the Lord and David. Then Mephibosheth said to the king, **Rather, let him** (Ziba) **take it all, inasmuch as my lord the king has come back in peace** (victory) **to his own house.** (2 Samuel 19:30) Mephibosheth was willing to give his entire estate to Ziba. His joy in life was in simply seeing David alive and returned to the throne.

The Zibas of Life

David saw the two reactions to the situations of life in Mephibosheth and Ziba. Both were left with nothing after the defeat and death of Saul. When David became king, he could have killed them both, but he treated them with grace. Mephibosheth was given an estate. Ziba, his sons and servants, were given employment and great benefits. For seventeen years, both had time to reflect on the goodness of David and the Lord. Despite his handicap, Mephibosheth became happy and confident. And though he had riches, he did not let them control him. Mephibosheth's happiness came from the Lord and his knowledge of God's Word. He would have been happy with or without his inheritance.

Ziba, on the other hand, had become bitter and ungrateful. He became greedy for the possessions of his new master and angry at the new king. He plotted to gain the wealth he oversaw each day. His happiness would come with more land, wealth and power. Ziba had mistakenly assumed possessions would bring him joy and missed the greatest lesson in life – happiness and joy can only come from a relationship with the Lord and a daily foundation in His Word. Possessions can only be truly enjoyed, when happiness is generated from a relationship with God.

When David saw this tragedy in Ziba, he recognized a great key to success in his own life. Like Mephibosheth, David had found joy and contentment outside of the details and possessions of life. People like David run into the Zibas of life every day in the office, in the church, in the classroom and everywhere people come together. They seemingly advance at the expense of the innocent and have the ear of those in charge.

God's plan for leadership and advancement is not with the Zibas of life. It is with the Mephibosheths and Davids. This is the story behind Psalm 131.

Chapter Two

Promotion Comes By Degrees

Psalm 131
A Song of Degrees of David

L ord, my heart is not haughty,
Nor my eyes lofty.
Neither do I concern myself with great matters,
Nor with things too profound for me.

2 Surely I have calmed and quieted soul,
Like a weaned child with his mother;
Like a weaned child is my soul within me.

3 O Israel, hope in the Lord
From this time forth and forever.

Those who
advance too
quickly because
of their own
efforts have
found the
descent to be
faster than the
ascent.

Psalm 131
A Song of Degrees of David

(*maalah*-advancements) of David

Time Is Really On Your Side

When seeking advancement, you may consider time as your enemy, but God gave you time as a friend and helper. Rapid growth brings more disillusionment than fulfillment. Time allows your character to develop along with your promotions. If your goal is promotion and prosperity, you will lose what you seek to gain.

Proverbs 23:4, 5:

> Labour not to be rich...for riches certainly make themselves wings; they fly away as an eagle toward heaven.

Seek the wisdom and strength of character, and promotion and prosperity will come. (Matthew 6:33) If advancement takes a little longer, thank the Lord for the extra time. It means that when the promotion arrives, you will be more patient, wiser and more capable of keeping what you have attained.

Ziba probably did not start out with an evil heart. Possibly he allowed it to develop over many years. He probably became frustrated with the slowness of promotion in his earlier years, and went about to advance himself.

You do not have to be an evil unbeliever like Ziba to fall into the self-promotion trap. Many Christians try it every day by attempting to help God in His plan for their life. "God's plan is too slow, I'll help Him," many say. This has to be the height of arrogance. Such a plan assumes that you know more than God. This is not only arrogance, it's blasphemy.

Once while taxiing in a 727 on the Dallas/Fort Worth runway, I saw a Concorde jet also waiting to take off. We were waiting to leave for Detroit, and the supersonic jet was waiting for clearance to leave for Paris. In about the same amount to time it would take us to fly to Detroit, the Concorde would travel across the ocean to France. I suddenly became frustrated while sitting in my seat. Why doesn't our government allow our aircraft companies to produce a supersonic jet? Why should the Europeans have one up on us? We invented the airplane anyway. We could have built an even better one...I thought.

While flying to Detroit, I couldn't get the Concorde out of my mind. It was flying three times faster than we were and I didn't like it one bit. I wanted this plane to fly that fast. Then the Lord spoke to me, "What are you going to do, get out and push?" I had to laugh at myself. I might as well sit back and enjoy the ride.

Trying to help God's plan in your life is like trying to get out and push a flying jet. You can't help, you will just end up getting hurt. But how many Christians have hurt themselves by getting out to push? They have tried to speed up the will of God by putting their own ideas and efforts into God's existing plan.

Promotion comes by degrees. Psalm 131 begins with this phrase to let us know that any rank in life comes over a period of time. God is smart in allowing promotion to come slowly. Those who advance too quickly because of their own efforts or talents have found the descent to be faster than the ascent. Slow growth allows us to learn valuable lessons on the way up, so once we reach the top, we can stay there and truly enjoy all the benefits.

David Had Failures

David probably saw traces of Ziba in himself. He also probably thought about where he might have been if he would have allowed his impatience to rule his life. In other words, David saw the importance of promotion by "degrees."

However, David's life was not without the sins of impatience, arrogance and self-promotion. Not only was he impatient at times, so were his followers who became weary of waiting on Samuel's prophecy to come to pass as they waited for David to take the throne. (I Samuel 16:1-13) David and his army forgot God would bring it to pass. They had forgotten the Lord is the author and finisher, the beginning and ending, the Alpha and Omega. They also forgot, **"...He who began a good work in you will perfect it."** (Philippians 1:6 NAS)

While running from Saul, David must have thought he experienced a setback rather than advancement. The desert was worse than being at home with the sheep, and he would have probably given anything to go home and sleep in his old bed. But if he would have done this, Saul could have found and killed him. David had gone from being a shepherd boy to a hero in Israel after killing Goliath. He then became the king's armorbearer and married Saul's daughter. After this, because of Saul's jealousy, he became an enemy of the nation, and the armies who had rejoiced at David's defeat over Goliath, were now chasing him through the deserts of Judea. What looked like a setback was a chance to watch God's delivering power. But it is difficult during a time like this to be patient and not try to help the plan of God.

Your Sins Hurt Others

In one situation, David tried to hide with the priests at Nob. (I Samuel 21) When David was alone and without a weapon, he remembered Goliath's sword was wrapped in the priest's linen ephod in Nob. Then when he came there, he lied to the priests to gain the sword's possession. He should have remembered, this sword did not help Goliath. But when a believer is carnal and tries to add his own strength to the hand of the Lord, he loses his spiritual perception. David could not think. Before he left Nob, he was spotted by Doeg, one of the kings spies. Then after David left, the king's army rode into Nob and killed the priests and their families. Only one remained to bring David the bad news.

David's sin of impatience led to the slaying of many innocent priests of the Lord. When David left Nob, he still was not thinking. He quickly walked into Gath, the hometown of Goliath. David actually went into enemy territory with Goliath's sword! He was surrounded by the enemy and about to be slain before he finally came to his senses and gave the situation to the Lord. His life was spared when he acted like a madman, scratched on the door, and slobbered into his beard. The Philistines thought he was insane and let him go.

Eventually, David ended up in the cave of Adullam with his career almost ended. (I Samuel 22) His mistakes had killed many innocent priests and brought him near to death himself. And, he had no one to blame but himself. Finally, David repented and became patient with God's plan.

David Had Successes

David learned from his failures to wait upon the Lord. It would be a long time before he took the throne of Israel. But still, he was willing to let the Lord bring this about in His own divine time. David had other opportunities to act in his own strength before his coronation, but he had learned very quickly to let the Lord handle them.

In one instance, while Saul and his army slept, David came into the camp, took the king's spear and a cruse of water, then quietly left. (I Samuel 26) Once outside the camp, he shouted to Saul from a nearby hilltop and told him what he had done. When Saul realized David could have easily killed him with his own spear, he was shocked into a humble gratitude. Sadly, it did not last. Saul had acted toward David with evil, and David returned it with unusual kindness.

In another instance, David's men had an opportunity to kill Saul while he was in a cave, but David restrained them from doing so. He would not be responsible for killing the king of Israel. David had learned to wait on the Lord and would take the throne of Israel in God's determined time.

Then while king, David's son, Absalom, revolted against his father, won the hearts of the people, and tried to take the throne. At this stage of his life, David wanted only to pray to see if he was still anointed to be Israel's king. He had learned that nothing he could do as a natural response could alter God's overall plan, and he knew that only God Who put him on the throne, could keep him there. As a result, David saw Absalom defeated and his throne restored, but the lessons that kept him while this came to pass were not learned overnight.

Promotion, prosperity and favor come one step, or one degree, at a time. John writes in his third epistle, **Beloved, I pray that you may prosper in all things and be in health, just as your soul prospers.** (3 John 2) But our soul does not prosper overnight. It happens a little at a time, **...precept upon precept...line upon line; here a little, and there a little.** (Isaiah 28:10)

Mark tells us the seed (the Word of God) that falls into good ground (our open heart) produces **"some thirtyfold, some sixty, and a some a hundred."** (Mark 4:20) Later in that same chapter we learn the seed produces, **...first the blade, then the head, after that the full grain in the head**. (Mark 4:28) Spiritual growth comes by degrees with natural promotion and prosperity increasing with it.

At David's death, he was a wiser and more popular king than he was at the beginning. And since he had learned to be patient through waiting on God, he could quickly recognize the lack of it in Ziba. For unlike Ziba, David had learned the lessons of his failures. As he watched Mephibosheth and Ziba react to the differing circumstances of their lives, he saw the lessons confirmed in their actions. One became impatient and bitter; the other, longsuffering and stable. One turned his weaknesses over to the Lord; the other tried to solve his own problems.

David observed and learned from these two men, and the event remained etched in his memory for years. As a result, four secrets of leadership were recognized by David that he will now share with us.

Chapter Three

Leadership Begins
in the Heart

Psalm 131

L ord, my heart is not haughty,
  Nor my eyes lofty.
    Neither do I concern myself with great matters,
    Nor with things too profound for me

Arrogance is
a disease that
makes everyone
sick except the
one who has it.

Psalm 131
A Song of Degrees of David

(*maalah*-advancements) of David

Verse one in Psalm 131 begins a series of four principles for success that king David had proven in his life. Whether you are a king, business manager, pastor or head of a household, these principles are timeless and will always work.

David is the best possible example of a man who did many things wrong and was not judged by God for his actions, but instead, was judged for his heart. If God had to make a choice, He would rather our actions be wrong and our hearts be right, than our hearts to be wrong and our actions right. He rebuked Israel many times in the Old Testament for their hardness of heart.

The people said they loved Him with their lips and actions, but their hearts were far from Him. (Isaiah 29:13) It is for this reason that David is a mystery to many believers today. His many sins, yet special place in God's heart, confuse many. Despite his episode with the priests at Nob, Bathsheba and a score of other sinful escapades, David was still called **"a man after God's own heart."** (1 Samuel 13:14) Why? He was quick to repent and seek the face of God. And once he endured the Lords' chastening for his futile shortcomings, he always rose higher than before. In fact, David learned from his sinful mistakes and made great improvements in life. These lessons made him a better person, and a better king. He maintained that longing, honest, seeking heart God had found when David was still tending sheep. And he maintained a heart after God. **"...man looks on the outward appearance, but the Lord looks at the heart."** (1 Samuel 16:7)

David understood that sin begins in the heart, not with actions. He also understood that to keep the heart pure is to keep the life pure. Actions and words are easier to keep in check if the heart is right before God.

Proverbs 4:23-27:

Keep your heart with all diligence,
For out of it spring the issues of life.
Put away from you a deceitful mouth,
And put perverse lips far from you.

Let your eyes look straight ahead,
And your eyelids look right before you.

Ponder the path of your feet,
And let all your ways be established.

Do not turn to the right or the left;
Remove your foot from evil.

David's First Secret: FREEDOM FROM ARROGANCE

Lord, my heart is not haughty (Hebrew-*gvowmah*-proud, arrogant), **nor my eyes lofty** (Hebrew-*ruwm*-looking for ways to self promotion)...

David's first success principle for us has to do with arrogance. Arrogance is the source of Lucifer's original sin (Isaiah 14:12-14, Ezekiel 28:16), and is the source of all personal sin in a believer's life. The original Hebrew language in Proverbs 16:18 says, **"Pride goes before destruction, and an haughty spirit before a fall."** Arrogance is simply exaggerated self-esteem. This root cause of sin puts the arrogant into competition with everyone around them. It causes them to condescend to those they consider beneath them, and to be jealous of those who seem better.

The arrogant must continually show they are better than everyone and try to keep every situation firmly in their control. They are too proud to admit their own weaknesses or recognize anyone else's strengths.

The arrogant tell the woman how to be a better housewife, the businessman how to better manage his company, the computer operator how to assess the newest technology, the football player how to pass or tackle, and the auto mechanic how to better tune an engine. They are experts at teaching others, but are unteachable themselves. How can you teach someone who knows everything?

Arrogant people consider themselves God's gift to the whole world. Arrogance is a disease that makes everyone sick except the one who has it.

The Arrogant and the Confident

The enemy of the arrogant is the relaxed, self-confident person. The Zibas of life do not understand the Mephibosheths or Davids. Just like Lucifer is toward God, the arrogant have a blatant disregard for authority because they consider themselves better than those in charge. They go over their boss's head to the president. They lie about those in authority and work both sides of any situation for their own good. Ziba had no idea that Mephibosheth would have given him part of his inheritance, if only he would have asked. Then after all the deception and lies, Mephibosheth offered it all to Ziba.

People who are truly secure know that the God Who gave, can give again. They also know that people who steal will not be happy. David and Mephibosheth didn't gain their happiness from things. Possessions do not bring happiness. David was happy when he watched over his father's sheep. He was happy living in a cave when on the run from Saul and his army. And because David's happiness came from the Lord, he was a mystery to Ziba.

Ziba probably thought David to be simpleminded and ignorant of the true ways of life. Yet David was very perceptive and well practiced in all of life's ways. As king, David witnessed many around him trying to promote themselves into positions that were only God-given. He had seen many Zibas, and would see them again.

Enemies of God

The reason the arrogant never stay ahead is because they fight against the Lord. Not only do the arrogant consider themselves smarter than everyone around them, they also secretly consider themselves smarter than God. In so doing, they appoint themselves as God's enemy. But God loves true humility in a person. He hates pride and conceit. The original Hebrew language in Proverbs 3:34 says, **"God sets Himself in battle array against the arrogant, but gives grace to the humble."** These were the words of David given to Solomon. They were success principles handed down from one generation to the next.

True Humility

Some struggle with how David was able to recognize his own humility. Critics say, "If you can admit your own humility, are you truly humble?" And, "Isn't admitting humility a sign of arrogance?" They have made the issue contradictory by saying humility is a virtue to be obtained, but that the humble person obtaining it should not recognize it or let others know. This comes from a misunderstanding of arrogance. David was not arrogant. He was confident. The proud mistake arrogance for confidence, and the humble mistake confidence for arrogance.

47

Confidence recognizes virtue, but it quickly gives credit to those who contributed to its development. Confident people credit partners, teachers, friends and the Lord for making them who they are. They believe anyone can obtain the virtues developed in their life. The arrogant, on the other hand, believe they have always had these virtues and assume the role as teachers of others. But they believe few can attain to their level.

It was freedom from arrogance that made David a true leader. People enjoyed his presence and felt uplifted when they left. He could truly give to the poor and receive from the rich. He was relaxed around both the uneducated and the wise. And all of David's praise went directly to the Lord, Whom he knew had made him a success, and Who would continue to promote him.

David's Second Secret: DELEGATION

Neither do I concern (involve) **myself with great matters,**
Nor with things too profound for me (Hebrew-*pala*-matters beyond my own ability).

This second leadership lesson of David in Psalm 131 says that freedom from arrogance allows the boss, manager, supervisor, secretary, or parent to delegate. The ability to delegate begins in the heart.

Arrogant people try to delegate, but it doesn't work. It doesn't work because they can't trust anyone else. They hire the best accountants, programmers and artists money can buy, but they are intimidated and jealous by their talents and even their very presence. They constantly watch over others shoulders to make sure everyone's work is to their liking. The arrogant stifle creativity in others. The people who work for them feel unnecessary. Why work for someone who thinks they can do it better themselves? If an arrogant person were truly honest, they would not hire talented people. They would hire inadequate workers off the streets and teach them to do it their way.

Strengths and Weaknesses

In verse one of Psalm 131, David admits he does not know everything and that many things are too high for him. He admits that many subjects in life are over his head so he does not involve himself in them. He was not afraid to admit his own weaknesses. David was gifted by God in certain areas, and understood those areas in which he was not. A wise man knows his strengths and weaknesses and searches out those who can make up the difference in his deficiencies. A wise man realizes the importance of teamwork. Wise David assembled a great team and was not jealous of men greater than himself. He did not have to seek out prosperity. Prosperity searched for him.

As a pastor, I have witnessed many ministers and congregational members working in certain areas where God has not gifted them. The lesson of David would say you are as much not gifted by God as you are gifted. It would also say that you will only succeed when you work on your areas of strength. Learn to rely on the gifts of others to fulfill the areas in which you are weak. Too often we desire to be "well rounded," but end up ineffective instead. No one can do everything well.

In my own ministry, I have envied other ministers who could do other things well. I am gifted to teach and pastor, but the gifts of an evangelist are not found in me. I have even prayed for these gifts, but I discovered after praying I just taught better. I realized one day that the Holy Spirit will only cultivate what He has given me. He will not give me someone else's ministry or gifts. This is why we need the entire body of Christ.

Stop the Buck Pass the Credit

A humble man like David will not only accept responsibility for his mistakes and wrong decisions, but he also won't care who gets the credit for an accomplishment. Like David, he knows that by sharing credit, others are strengthened, and that when a team is stronger, the leader becomes stronger. This circle of power continues to increase.

In the books of First and Second Chronicles, lists of skilled musicians, writers, craftsmen and architects are given. An arrogant man would never list them. He would only give any available credit to himself. But David not only listed them, he used and trusted them. So they, in turn, gladly served and trusted him.

Once when David's men risked their own lives behind enemy lines just to get their leader a drink from the well of Bethlehem, he was so moved with gratitude and admiration that he wouldn't drink the water. He poured it out as an offering to the Lord. (2

Samuel 23:15-17) Because David honored those who served him, those who served him honored David.

Humility and delegation are two of the most important secrets of David's success. This is how he conquered large armies with only a few highly motivated and greatly dedicated men.

These two secrets alone could make you a great leader, but David is not through yet. There are two more powerful secrets in this "psalm of degrees" that are just as life-changing.

Chapter Four

The Witness of a Child

Psalm 131

L ord, my heart is not haughty,
Nor my eyes lofty.
Neither do I concern myself with great matters,
Nor with things too profound for me.

2 Surely I have calmed and quieted soul,
Like a weaned child with his mother;
Like a weaned child is my soul within me.

Emotions
are the Spice
of Life

Psalm 131
A Song of Degrees of David

(*maalah*—advancements) of David

David's Third Secret: CONQUERING THE TEMPER

Surely (behold) **I have calmed** (Hebrew-*shavah*-equalized) **and quieted** (Hebrew-*damam*-composed) **my soul, Like a weaned child with** (beside) **his mother; Like a weaned child is my soul within me.** (Psalm 131:2)

This verse reveals that David learned to control his emotions. From Bible sources, we know that he was a redheaded, freckled man. And though the temper of redheads is a widely known stereotype, we do have examples of David's emotional outbursts in scripture.

For example, after David had sinned with Bathsheba, he was confronted by Nathan the prophet. After hearing Nathan's ewe lamb analogy, David burst out in anger. Then in fiery indignation he declared that the man who had committed this insensitive act would surely die, and that he would have to pay recompense fourfold. (2 Samuel 12:5, 6) Of course David had no idea that story was about him. But once he did, he was quick to repent. One of David's biggest challenges must have been to overcome his quick temper.

Emotions

Emotions can be a great blessing, or a wicked curse in life. Emotions are often seen as evil, but they are given by God. Emotions can't be evil if they come from our heavenly Father. God Himself has emotions. When emotions are put in their proper place, under our control, they can serve us as a blessing. But when emotions control us, they can become a frustrating curse.

The Spice of Life

Emotions provide the spice of life. Without spices, food would be dull. Spices give everyday food a variety of wonderful tastes, but we could not live by their flavors alone. They are only meant to flavor our food. In the same way, emotions are not meant to be lived by. They are meant to give flavor and excitement to everyday life. Without them, life would be dull.

Some emotions can act as an alarm, giving us warnings in life. Much like pain tells us to remove our hand from a hot pan or sharp nail, fear warns us to approach an oncoming circumstance with caution. Of course, we do not live our life under the control of fear, but neither should we disregard its message when it comes. Fear is an emotion that can protect our lives.

Emotions are also the great appreciators and responders of life. They cause us to react to pleasing and stimulating circumstances. Crying, laughing and shouting are all emotions we share with God Himself. And since was have been made in His image, we should use our God-given emotions in the same way that He does. God's emotions are appreciators of and responders to both righteousness and sin in the earth. God controls His emotions, and we should do the same.

Our life should be controlled by God's Word and by the power of the Holy Spirit. They give us the ability to dominate and control our emotions. Having one's emotions under control is a great mark of maturity. Such control can bring us into great stability and security—the kind of stability exhibited by David.

Evil emotions are a sin and should be treated as such. We would certainly ask God to forgive us for stealing, lying or committing adultery. Then we would proceed to put it out of our lives, knowing that those sins are not pleasing to God. But if we happen to have anger or bitterness, we usually put up with it thinking, *This is just part of my personality. I can do nothing about it. I can't change who I am.* But listen to the words of Paul, **Let all bitterness, wrath, anger, clamor** (the display of anger), **and evil speaking be put away from you, with all malice** (evil intentions). (Ephesians 4:31) Now notice how Paul in Colossians 3:8, 9 mentions emotions along with the sins of lying and blasphemy. **But now you yourselves are to put off these things: anger, wrath, malice, blasphemy, filthy language out of your mouth. Do not lie to one another...**

Just as you have the power to put away evil emotions, you can also yield to emotions that bless both you and others. **And be kind to one another, tenderhearted, forgiving one another...** (Ephesians 4:32). **Therefore, as the elect of God, holy and beloved,** put on tender mercies, kindness, humility, meekness, longsuffering...** (Colossians 3:12)

A Child as an Example

The issue in verse two of Psalm 131 is anger under control. David had come to the place of a nursing child in his emotional life. An infant child has no anger. Just try to insult a baby and you will probably get a smile or a laugh. Call a child an evil name, and you will probably get the same reaction. David had to learn to keep his emotions consistent in all situations, and he did. The longer David lived, the more composed he became. In other words, David grew older in wisdom and younger in anger.

In his daily affairs of the kingdom, David could listen to criticism without feeling threatened. Unlike many believers, he did not have a chip on his shoulder waiting from someone to knock it off. He could separate his criticism from himself. Many people, when criticized, take the criticism personally. To criticize their work, ideas or decisions, is to criticize them. They can't see the good a person is trying to contribute, and take the advice as a personal attack. But David passed this point of stifled maturity and became as a nursing child when criticized. He had learned to recognize the difference between constructive criticism and a critical attitude.

Jesus and Paul on Becoming Like Children

Jesus told His disciples, **Let** (allow) **the little children come to Me, and do not forbid them; for of such is the kingdom of heaven.** (Matthew 19:14) The Greek word for "little children" (*paidion*) means a *very little child*. I do not believe this verse is only speaking of entering the new birth. Although we must have faith as a little child and accept what is given to us from God, we must also become childlike as we grow in our spiritual life. We need to be mature in our knowledge of God, but childlike with anger and bitterness.

If there was ever a New Testament congregation that was ruled by their emotions, it was the Corinthian church. They had become excited over spiritual gifts, but indifferent toward the ministry and application of God's Word. Paul instructed them **Brethren, do not be children in understanding; however, in malice (wickedness) be babes, but in understanding be mature** (1 Corinthians 14:20). We are never to remain children in knowledge, understanding and wisdom.

We are to grow. However, in anger and revenge, we, like David, are to learn to be as little children.

Older and Wiser?

Many say that old age brings on a more mellow attitude. But this is not true. Old age is not a guarantee for a more tolerant attitude toward others in life. Knowledge and application of scriptural principles are what bring consistency and more composure in daily life. Many of the meanest and most angry people are old. Contentment does not come over a period of time. It is not based on circumstances. Contentment is learned. As Paul said, **...I have learned in whatever state I am, to be content** (Philippians 4:11) The issue in this verse is anger under control. It doesn't just happen naturally.

Like Paul, David grew in God's Word through the years and continued to apply godly principles as he grew older. Emotions should not rule a nation, a business, a family or a personal life. This should only be done by the Word of God. But emotions should be able to appreciate the result.

For example, when David brought the ark back to Jerusalem in accordance with the instruction of God's

Word, he rejoiced and danced before it. (2 Samuel 6:15) In fact, he was so emotional that his wife Michal criticized him for uncovering himself**...as one of the base fellows shamelessly uncovers himself!** (v. 20) But this is how David had learned to live and rule in Israel. His emotions did not rule his kingly decisions, they simply provided his spice for life.

Now, just as the guests commented at the first miracle of Jesus that the best wine had been held to the end, the most powerful and best kept secret of David will now be revealed. God always saves His best for last.

Chapter Five

Truth Never Dies

Psalm 131

Lord, my heart is not haughty,
Nor my eyes lofty.
Neither do I concern myself with great matters,
Nor with things too profound for me.

2 Surely I have calmed and quieted soul,
Like a weaned child with his mother;
Like a weaned child is my soul within me.

3 O Israel, hope in the Lord
From this time forth and forever.

David became a
king of kings
to all kings
after him.

Psalm 131
A Song of Degrees of David

(*maalah*-advancement) of David

David's Fourth Secret:
FOLLOWING THOSE WHO WENT BEFORE

O Israel, hope (remain) **in the Lord
From this time forth and forever.** (Psalm 131:3)

In order to properly understand verse three of our psalm, we have to see it as a continuation of verses one and two. In the first two verses, David uses himself as an example for Israel to follow. Now in verse three he asks Israel to ultimately follow the One Who influenced his own personal life more than any other. He asks his followers to follow the Lord.

In this verse David asks nothing more than that the Lord be seen through his own life. He was not afraid to tell Israel what the apostle Paul told the Corinthians, **Imitate me, just as I also imitate Christ.** (1 Corinthians 11:1, Philippians 3:17)

David had also been influenced by the godly Hebrew patriarchs. His life had been molded and changed by the testimonies of Bible leaders such as Abraham, Jacob, Joseph and Moses. Like David, these heroes had their own failures and successes. Their testimonies ultimately told David to follow the Lord. Now David's name could be added to the list of heroes for Israel to follow. The Lord is to be followed, but so is the godly example of David. This is the meaning of verse three.

Even the world around us knows the importance of good examples. The study of history brings forth many heroes that help to keep our focus clear and life on track. Military heroes are studied by our servicemen to find the courage to fight for our freedom. Sports heroes are studied and used to help players and sports teams win. And business tycoons and visionaries are studied to help keep employees motivated.

As believers, we also need to surround ourselves with motivating examples. The Bible is filled with them. We can compare our successes and failures with theirs, knowing that the God Who brought them through, will do the same for us. We also need to search out godly people around us to look to as living examples. Spiritual heroes did not cease to exist when the Bible was completed. Heroes can still be found in the home, the office, on the assembly line, and in the church. God has not hidden Himself in heaven. He is still making Himself known through daily heroes in life. **Do not become lazy, but imitate those who through faith and patience inherit the promises.** (Hebrews 6:12) The bottom line in any profession always looks better when we compare ourselves to heroes.

As king, David had an inspirational hall of fame that came from the annals of God. In David's lineage were military and national leaders who had carved out the nation of Israel against impossible odds. And since David was king, commander in chief, chief musician and prophet, he surrounded himself with God's historical heroes from all these areas of life. He used their examples to make daily decisions in his courts and battlefields.

When David came to the end of his life, he became an example too. Like those who went before him, David was inducted into God's hall of fame. (Hebrews 11:32) He knew well the lesson of life that teaches life comes to an end, but the truth of it never dies. The examples he left would be used by citizens of Israel as well as other nations for generations to come. David's voice still speaks. *You are studying his psalm today.*

David: A King of Kings

Although David's life on earth was wonderful, what happened through his death was even greater. God had a plan for this king that David himself would not have believed. I personally believe God had to keep it a secret while David was alive, because if David would have known about it, he could not have accepted it. It would have been difficult to handle such incredible love.

God would use David as "the" example to be followed by the kings of Israel from his day on. He would become a king of kings to all kings after him. Each king after David had the same Scriptures, the same Holy Spirit and the same list of godly examples. But they would have one example more. They would have the life of David to look at as "the" model of successful leadership. David's example would go down in the biblical record as Israel's standard for kingly rule. Let's look at some of Israel's kings who ruled after David's death to see who used his example, and who did not.

Solomon 1000 BC

One generation later, *Solomon* began his reign by beseeching God for His wisdom, but he never matured as his father David. **For it was so, when Solomon was old, that his wives turned his heart after other gods; and his heart was not loyal to the Lord his God, as *was the heart of his father David.*** (1 Kings 11:4)

Asa 912–872 BC

Asa, who ruled a few hundred years after David's death, was a blessing to Israel. **Asa did what was right in the eyes of the Lord, *as did his father David*** (ancestor). (1 Kings 15:11)

Amaziah 803–775 BC

Amaziah ruled many hundreds of years after David. He grew in the ways of the Lord. But he never reached to David's level. **And he (Amaziah) did what was right in the sight of the Lord, *yet not like his father David...***2 Kings 14:3)

Ahaz 741–726 BC

Ahaz took the throne at twenty years of age and ruled sixteen years. But he served Israel in an evil way and was destroyed as a result. **Ahaz was twenty years old when he became king, and reigned sixteen years in Jerusalem; and he did not do what was right in the sight of the Lord his God,** *as his father David had done.* (2 Kings 16:2)

Hezekiah 726–697 BC

Hezekiah came to the throne three hundred years after David, took full advantage of the Word of God, and matured greatly. **And he** (Hezekiah) **did what was right in the sight of the Lord,** *according to all that his father David had done.* (2 Kings 18:3)

Jehoshaphat 874–850 BC

Jehoshaphat ruled the people well. Now the Lord was with Jehoshaphat, *because he walked in the former ways of his father David;* **he did not seek the Baals.** (2 Chronicles 17:3)

73

Josiah 639–608 BC

Josiah was another great king over Israel. **And he (Josiah) did what was right in the sight of the Lord,** *and walked in the ways of his father David;* **he did not turn aside to the right hand or the left. …and in the twelfth year he began to purge Judah and Jerusalem of the high places, the wooden images, the carved images, and the molded images.** (2 Chronicles 34:2, 3)

As you can see, the Davidic line spanned a time period of almost five hundred years. And astonishingly, the kings were not only commanded to follow the Lord, they were commanded to follow David as well. The Lord is perfect, David was not. Of course the kings had an ultimate goal set before them to be like the Lord, but they also had a natural example set before them in King David. Why? Because David had learned to overcome his own imperfections and maintain a heart after God.

I'm sure God must have looked at David's sins and shook His head in sorrow. I'm just as sure He must have looked at David's repentance and nodded His head approvingly. I can see Him smiling as He said, "I love that guy. In fact, I love him so much, I want all of Israel's kings from now on to study him and use his life as an example."

The kings after David who failed, all failed for the same reasons, just as the kings who succeed after him, all succeeded for the same reason. They either followed or rejected the Word of God and David's example. The principles of God's Word and His Holy Spirit do not change from generation to generation. They are constant and will always work, as they did in that day.

A Greater King Followed After David

The greatest testimony of David's example to his following generations is Israel's Messiah-King, the Lord Jesus Christ, Who would also come from the lineage of David. He would represent God's greatest stamp of approval on David's methods of rulership and his heart of maturity. The following commendation is found one psalm later, in another song of degrees.

Psalm 132:8-11:

Arise (rise up), **O Lord, to Your resting place** (the place of your habitation), **You and the ark of Your strength.**

Let Your priests be clothed with righteousness, And let Your saints shout for joy (celebrate with shouting).

For Your servant David's sake, Do not turn away the face of Your Anointed (Messiah—Jesus Christ).

The Lord has sworn in truth to David; He will not turn from it: I will set (establish) **upon Your throne** (David's) **the fruit of your body.**

These verses speak of Israel, the priestly nation of God, and that out of this nation, God would send Israel's greatest King, His Messiah, the Lord Jesus. They say that God would not be slack, but would keep His Word concerning the coming of His Redeemer. And that He would offer rest to the ones who put their trust in the Lord. This rest would eventually come to the whole earth, so this verse is not only Messianic, it is millennial. Through the lineage of David, God's place of habitation would not longer be in an earthly tabernacle or temple. It would be in the hearts of those who believe in Him.

The Old Testament ark that contained the mercy seat, showed us that the direction of our spiritual reference was to always be pointed toward the justice of God. This justice was fulfilled on the cross through the sprinkling of blood, as the place of God's propitiation. It spoke of God's coming satisfaction through the work of His Son that would eventually redeem all who would believe in Him and accept His work.

The priests in these verses are not only the Old Testament priesthood of Aaron, they are the new priests of the New Testament. It would be the coming church that would serve under the Great High Priesthood of the Lord Jesus Christ. The righteousness they would possess would cause them to rejoice, celebrate and shout!

In other words, this song of degrees takes us from the rule of King David over God's natural kingdom, to the reign of God's Messiah over His spiritual kingdom. After David died, there would be a long line of natural kings, good and bad. But the eventual King in David's line would be the virgin born Son of God, Who would become mankind's sacrifice and the Creator of the Church, a kingdom of royal priests.

A Promise Which Cannot Be Broken

Psalm 89:3, 4:

> I have made a covenant with My chosen (David), I have sworn to My servant David: Your seed I will establish *forever*, And build up your throne to *all generations*, Selah.

God gave David the promise and guarantee of a Messiah-King Who would come forth from Him. Although many in David's lineage did not follow the Lord, God continued to keep His promise because of David's heart. God blessed David because he saw in him the attributes of His Son. David's historical impact would not only be seen in the kings of Judah over the next five hundred years, it would be seen forever, because of David's heart. As God promised,

2 Samuel 7:12, 13:

> When your days are fulfilled and you rest sleep
> with your fathers, I will set up your seed after
> you, who will come form your body, and I will
> establish his kingdom. He shall build a house for
> My name, and I will establish the throne of his
> kingdom forever.

These verses tell us God loved David so much
that the historical impact of David's heart on God
would provide a promise that could not be broken.
This promise, now partially fulfilled, brought the first
coming of Jesus through the virgin birth, and with
Him, the age of the Church. In its completion, the
promise will bring the second coming of Jesus and
His millennial reign.

In 2 Samuel 7:12-13, the Lord promised to sit on the
throne of David, and to do this (out of David's seed),
by becoming a human being. This is the promise
of the incarnation. Through this divinely promised
offspring would come the long awaited union of God
and man. The promise said that after He ascended to
David's throne, He would never leave it; that this King
would be even better than David because He would

be perfect and sinless. He would also be eternal and never die. Through His incarnation and possession of the throne, He would fulfill the "seed of the woman" spoken of in Genesis 3:15 and the "seed of David."

David is not asking for the Messiah to come because of his own faithfulness. He is asking because of God's faithfulness, Who promised He would come. David looks past his own mistakes and sins to remember God's Word. He is reminding God of His promise and of His integrity. David could become bold where the authority of God's Word was concerned. His example is powerfully ours.

Now please don't miss the impact of this psalm. David was not only an example for Israel's for Israel's kings to follow, he was also the standard that God the Father used for His Son, Jesus Christ. In essence, David became a king of kings, even to "The King" of kings. God would be pleased with His Son's humanity as He followed in the obedient footsteps and faithful heart of His servant, David the king.

Now this is truly an amazing thing. It is one thing for God to point to His Son, Jesus, as an example for men to follow. It is quite another for God to use a man as an example for your sons and others to follow. But it is something altogether astounding for the Father to use a man as an example for His own Son, the Lord Jesus, to follow.

Various commendations were given to other kings in David's line, but no king after David was ever given such credits and accolades as Jesus. **He** (Jesus) **will be great, and will be called the Son of the Highest; and the Lord God will give Him the throne of *His father David.*** (Luke 1:32)

Chapter Six

Are You Ready to be a King of Kings?

You Can Begin
to Write Your Own
Psalm of Degrees
for Others to
Follow.

Psalm 131
A Song of Degrees of David

(*maalah*-advancement) of David

Would Others Follow Your Example?

N ow is the time to ask yourself some questions. Would you consider yourself a king of kings? Have you come to a point in your life where you are an example to others? If a psalm of degrees were written about you, what would it say? Have you advanced and grown spiritually since you received Jesus as your Savior? Have you followed in the footsteps of David? More importantly, have you followed in the footsteps of Jesus?

You may not feel like you have any attributes Jesus Himself would want to follow, but what about other Christians around you? Do others look at your life and say, "I would like to be a Christian like him?" If they were praying for a natural example to respect and follow, would the Lord impress them to follow you?

What about your own family? Have you been an example to your mate and children? Like David, could your sons and daughters be known as "pleasers of the Lord, whose hearts were perfect as the heart of their father?"

It may be surprising to you, but the answer to all of these questions can be "yes."

If David stands at the top of the ladder of promotion, we need to study the steps that led him there. Anyone at the top had to begin at the bottom, and every journey begins with a first step. So if you feel you are on the lowest level, your first step can begin today. You can begin to write your own psalm of degrees for others to follow.

Step One:
GAIN AN UNDERSTANDING OF GRACE.

If there is any one message that runs throughout the Word of God, it is that our Father is a God of grace. Simply put, *grace is God's gift*. Your salvation and all of its blessings is a benevolent gift of God. Grace on your part cannot be worked for, earned or deserved. Knowing this can help you grow as David did as a man after God's own heart.

To become this person, you have to understand God's heart. David did. David understood that God was gracious and merciful long before the coming of Jesus. His psalms were filled with the grace and mercy of God. They tell us of the Lord's mercy that endures forever. (Psalm 136) Just as Jesus told us to "be merciful, even as your Father is merciful," and as Paul told us to "grow in grace," so do David's psalms in the Old Testament.

In the New Testament, the Pauline epistles not only contain teaching on grace, they usually begin with grace salutations and end with grace benedictions. How do you think your life would be changed if each day that you sought to grow in grace began and ended with thanksgivings of grace?

Step Two:
DO NOT TAKE YOURSELF TOO SERIOUSLY.

God always takes nobodies and makes somebodies of them. If He finds a somebody, He has to first take the time to make them a nobody before He can properly use them. Moses, the prime minister of Egypt, had to spend forty years in the wilderness tending sheep before God could send him back to Egypt as Israel's deliverer. Powerful Saul of Tarsus had to spend many years in seclusion before he reemerged as the apostle Paul. Both of these great leaders were renowned among their followers as very meek people.

A meek person doesn't take himself too seriously. That doesn't mean the meek don't take the Lord and their mission in life seriously. The meek are able to put things into perspective. They know God's mission was here before He called them and that it will be here long after they are gone. They also understand the task is important, but God could get anyone to do it.

Think about it. Someone handed the torch to you, and others will carry it when you are gone. The Zibas of life always think of themselves "more highly than they ought," but David always knew the battle and victory belonged to the Lord. You will take another step up when you realize this too.

Step Three:
MAINTAIN COMMUNION WITH GOD.

Daily communion produces strength. Just as David understood the importance of time with the Lord, you must recognize this too.

Communion includes first of all, time in God's Word. Through his "exceeding great and precious promises" you can partake of God's divine nature and escape the corruption of the world. (2 Peter 1:4)

Secondly, communion demands a daily prayer life. Needs and fellowship are the central purposes of prayer. "A" king of kings realizes his utter dependence on "The" King of kings and lets his "requests be made known unto God."

Finally, communion includes praise and worship. Thanksgiving and adoration are the result of a lifestyle of intimacy with God. Every Old and New Testament hero offered outpourings of praise to God. Why then would God require any less of you?

Step Four:
USE SUCCESSFUL PEOPLE AS EXAMPLES.

People who succeed in life follow the trail that other successful leaders have left behind. The Word of God, and history itself, are filled with people you can pattern yourself after. Bible study books should be supplemented with a good library of biographies and books on history. The history of our nation and the church are equally filled with men and women